WINNING SECRETS OF BEING

NUMBER #2

A PERSONAL SUCCESS GUIDE

By

TAYDO NICKSON

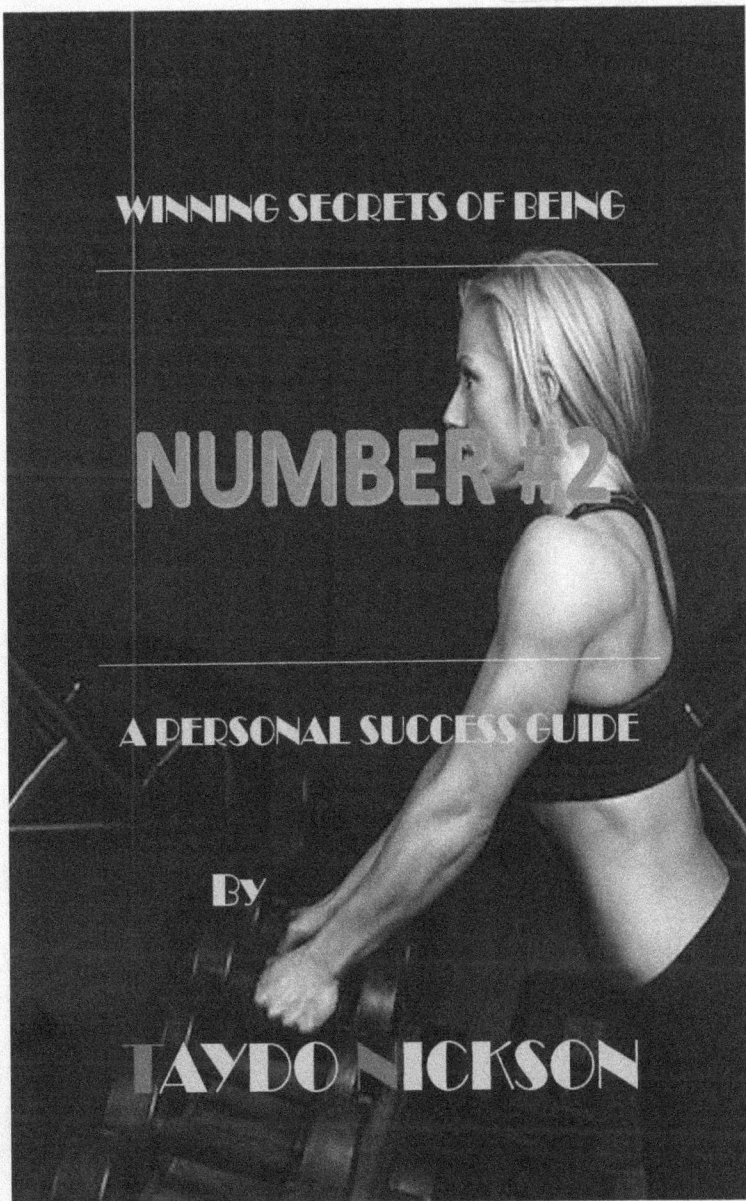

BEING NO.2
PERSONAL SUCCESS GUIDE

BY

TAYDO NICKSON

ISBN: 978-0-620-86126-7

WWW.XPONENTWORLD.COM

<u>DEDICATION</u>

To all those who want to succeed badly in a hopeless situation and ready for change.

We can do it, we must. God bless you in your life changing journey.

TABLE OF CONTENTS

Wise words from Jim Rohn......................... 11

Introduction........................ (12 – 16)

What this is all about

Aspire to be great

It's all about you.

Reconnect with your inner Child.

The Goals That Never Happen

How we're going to Fix Your Goal Setting and Help You to Start Living the Life of Your Dreams

What's in this book?

Disclaimer

A Quote from Jim Rohn......................17

Chapter 1: Goal setting and time is important for your success......... (18 – 22)

The Problem with Your Current Goals

What Good Goals Look Like

How to Formulate Your Goals

Time can be Converted or Transformed.

Time can be conserved.

Time is measured by created moments

Time is valuable.

A Quote from Bob Marley...........................23

Chapter 2: Study all the number ones in your field of choice......... (24 – 29)

Learn from the best in your field.

The golden task

So what is success really??

The Formula – How to Structure Goals and Make Your Plan

A Quote from Napoleon Hill.........................30

Chapter 3: Improve your Speech....................... (31 – 38)

You're the best but you have stage fright and shy.

Paint pictures with your words.

Learn how to ask informative questions.

Do not chase great moments or good feelings because they change all the time.

Your words have immeasurable power.

Choose statement and your words wisely.

Letting Go of Fear

How to know if you're Procrastinating?

Fear Setting

A Quote from Manuel L. Quezon.........39

CHAPTER 4: Be practical and keep up with the times.............. (40 – 45)

Be Practical.

Be careful of which task you make automatic in your life.

Keep up with the times.

Have a clear picture of your dream in mind.

How to Make Your Fitness Goals Happen

How to Set and Stick to Realistic Goals

A Quote from Robert T. Kiyosaki.............................46

CHAPTER 5: Find a way always and not excuses.......... (47 – 50)

How to Make Your Career Goals Happen

Knowing What You Want

Creating a Fool Proof Strategy

The Path of Least Resistance

The Fail Fast Model

A Quote from Xponent World.............51

CHAPTER 6: How to Make Your Relationship Goals Happen... (52 -54)

Taking Stock

Creating a Plan for Dating

Knowing What You Want

A Quote from Thato Moahlodi...................55

CHAPTER 7: The Power of Association........ (56 – 59)

Do not associate the things you love with pain.

Self-doubt is never worth it. It sprouts defeat.

Associating what you love with hard-work.

Associating things you love with the "I have to" mentality.

Here is the secret, you'll probably laugh when you read this.

How to Make Your Travel Goals Happen

Alternative Travel Strategies

A Quote from Unknown...............60

CONCLUSION...................61

It's time to make it happen no more excuses.

A Quote from Dwayne Johnson.........................62

NOTES
AUTOGRAPHS OF INSPIRING PEOPLE IN YOUR LIFE.

"LIFE IS LIKE COOKING EVERY DISH HAS ITS OWN INGREDIENTS. IMAGINE THE LIFE THAT YOU DESIRE TO LIVE, GO OUT, FIND THE PROPER INGREDIENTS AND COOK IT."

—

JIM ROHN

INTRODUCTION

What this is all about.

Being number two is a book that will teach you to win from the grounds you're currently in right now.

It is not a book for the lazy or even the faint hearted. It will teach you to have the superhero mentality.

It is written for those who are tired of their current state, the people who try and try and end up in the same situation with the same results in their hands.

They're frustrated, angry and bitter, never not even in a single day has the thought of quitting crossed their minds. You always have hope and a strong believe that things will change for the better.

Well, it will only be fair to tell you that we are facing a similar situation and I wrote this book for us and people with the same mentality as us.

I want it to be timeless and remain as a reminder of this day where you and I take an oath to do whatever's necessary to win and take the crown that belongs to us according to our abilities, if not, it is an oath to die trying and doing whatever it takes.

Aspire to be great.

In all my life I always aspire to be great. I aspire to act and not react in any given moment as well as inspire others.

As we all know, being the ultimate best is always a challenge. I spent the whole eighteen years waking up and grinding hard even with the knowledge that I am not at the peak of my success yet, I still wake up and get it done.

The key is not to do what the world requires you to do but do what you require of yourself always and forever.

Don't lose all you have because of letting other people to make tough decisions for you because this will strip you from your love, hope and your joy.

Do not kill your dreams by merely being lazy and by not having enough confidence in your capabilities and yourself.

Have a well-structured plan of your life and always get rid of all your lazy habits. As you know as well as I do that nothing is ever easy, so go and do it anyway.

You know the intense thing that I've learned over the years is that self-reliance is the way to go because, honestly, no one is more equipped to deal with all your nonsense but you. After all it's your nonsense.

Say this oath with me (I'm here to inflict change, learn and absorb all the positivity I can get, to get all that I want and be of help to others.). I swear that felt like an (Amen) moment.

Repeat it with **love**.

It's all about you.

The real truth about pursuing success is that it will cause you to take on a journey in a road of loneliness and face strong adversaries along the way.

Success will expose your fears and weaknesses as well as your victories, you will need tools like a strong belief in oneself, hope, passion, love and strong confidence and partnerships.

This will be a lonely road because no one in all God's world can see in the depth of your heart but you and everyone is planning to succeed in their lives as well.

So don't expect them to prioritise the achievement your desires.

You will be left there hurt and humiliated, with nothing but regret and a whole lot of what ifs but that does not mean it's the end and not to pursue success but it means the universe is toughening you up for what is to come.

I love what Jim Rohn had said in one of his famous speeches: "What do people have planned for you?? Not much." And as always he was right and he still is.

It's all about you and it is up to you to make your dreams possible and real. For sure you've heard this a lot, well keep it in your mind and heart because it is as true as breathing.

The big important questions in life that you need to keep on answering are: "Are you willing to change? Are you willing to do whatever it takes?" and "Do you really love yourself enough to pull through it all?"

Then again, it is not about your boss or that promotion at work you always wanted and that top grade at school that you studied hard for.

It's all about you taking good care of your whole self from your spirit to your body. You and your emotions are a priority and should always work in sync to achieve great exploits.

Always remember that you want peace of mind and love in your life and remember that you also want everlasting joy.

Reconnect with your inner Child.

To achieve greatness you need to revive your inner child. It must be the child who always loved, cared and believed in his/her dreams unconditionally. That inner child who is always ready to do whatever it takes to bring his/her imagination to life.

All I want you to do is close your eyes right now and try to search deep inside your soul. I want you to go way back to the age of seven because according to scientists that's the foundation age of the person you are today.

Go deeper and meditate remember all the moments, the people you used to hang out with, the toys you played with, the imaginary characters you always pretended to be with that always brought you joy and that's if you had one at the time, the love you've ever felt and the laughter.

Relive all these happy moments for a minute, an hour. It's entirely up to you. Just **Escape**.

By doing this you will find yourself discovering how you horrible or fun your childhood was. Even in the mist of all the problems you've had as a child, you will find out that you still enjoyed and loved every moment of your childhood.

Now try to think about the moments that birthed the situations you're in today, the moment where everything good or bad had begun. The twist of fate moment.

Reconnect with the inner child before he/she had the chance to grow up and try to answer some of the questions you never had a chance to answer at that time. Questions like: What have you done? Why did you do it? Was it worth it? And the like.

You'll find out that the answer to all these undeniable questions is that you've might have suppressed your true feelings of how you feel about yourself.

You pleased others in the expense of ignoring your true desires, you've always ignored the voice of the inner person and this caused the death of the prominent child, your true self.

You've given this horror a name eventually and you called it 'growing up'. Yes you heard me well, I said growing up.

Well I have nothing against growing up but what I have a problem with is how you intend to grow up and go into the future as. Who is the man in the mirror and who is the man inside? Are they the same?

People get it wrong with the concept of growing up. They intend to look at the outward person forgetting the inward person.

As the good book says "what will it benefit man if he acquires all the riches of the world and loses his soul?"

Reconnect with your soul, your inner man and revive your inner child and unlock the person you really are.

The Goals That Never Happen

How many incomplete goals do you currently have on your agenda? If you're anything like the vast majority of us, then chances are that you have hundreds of projects that you started and never completed, countless goals that you told your friends but never saw through and all kinds of dreams that seem to be getting less and less likely to come to fruition.

And it's for this reason, that you may find people roll their eyes when you tell them your 'next big project'. When you start a new training program to lose weight and everyone – including you – knows that you're likely to have lost interest by month two.

Or when you talk about the app you intend to make, the website, or the business project.

Or when you talk about that dream trip to Japan...

This is the way of things for many of us. We work incredibly hard at things we don't feel passionately about just to put food on the table but when it comes to fulfilling our dreams, we are remarkably ineffective.

It's time to change all that and to start making those goals happen. But how can you turn it all around?

How we're going to Fix Your Goal Setting and Help You to Start Living the Life of Your Dreams

Accomplishing goals is about strategy, it is about making a cognitive shift to change the way you're thinking and it's about being smart about how you approach each goal. It's also about knowing how to choose your goals and even how to phrase them.

This book is going to show you how to make those changes then. You'll learn how to choose and write goals effectively, how to write effective action plans and how to make sure you stick with your goals and never give up.

But this book is going to be a little different than most goal-setting tomes, too. After we've given you the broad tools you need to start setting and accomplishing your goals, we're then going to take a look at how you can begin to put them into practice.

Because while a goal can be pretty much anything, for many of us they are going to fall into one of a few different categories. Most of us have goals for our relationships, goals for our fitness, goals for our careers and goals for travel.

We're going to provide not only the abstract strategies you need to start making effective goals then, but also the step-to-step processes that will let you apply these strategies in each of these areas.

By the end of this book, you'll be adept at setting and accomplishing any goal. And at the same time, you'll have powerful strategies for improving your relationships, your fitness, your career and more.

Ready to change your life?

What's in this book?

This book will teach and walk you through these topics:

- Use your time wisely.
- Live in the present moment
- Learn to be clean
- Learn to understand.
- Study all the Number ones
- The power of association and
- Prepare yourself for greatness.

Read it throughout and savour every chapter and apply these teachings in your life.

Disclaimer

I do not guarantee success as it is totally dependent on an individual person and unique abilities they have. It's also advisable to seek medical or professional help when things are too heavy for you.

Be willing to learn and have an open mind. I believe you've taken the first step in self-love by purchasing and using this book for the greater good in your life which is its purpose.

Hope you enjoy the awesome journey! ☺

Yours in love

Taydo Nickson.

"If you are not willing to risk the <u>UNUSUAL</u>,

You will have to settle for the <u>ORDINARY</u>."

-

JIM ROHN

CHAPTER 1

Goal setting and time is important for your success.

Learning how to set goals properly is arguably the most powerful skill that you can possibly learn. Why? Because it will allow you to then accomplish a huge range of _other_ goals. When you know how to set goals, it allows you to effectively work toward anything. This is the key to unlocking pretty much everything you could want from life.

So ironically, the first goal you should focus on is the goal of setting goals!

And until now, you've probably been doing it all wrong...

The Problem with Your Current Goals

How can a goal be wrong?

Sure, any objective is a worthwhile one, but the way that you phrase your goals and structure them, is going to massively change your likelihood of finding success.

Let's take weight loss as an example because it's one of the more straightforward goals that is easiest to implement.

When you set out to lose weight, you should start with a concrete goal. And for most people this will look something like this: "Lose 2 stone by next year"

This is a terrible goal.

Why? First of all, it is far too vague. How are you losing weight? Weight from where? Why do you want to lose the weight? What do you actually want to look like?

At the same time, it's out of your control. Even if you are completely committed to your goal, you may find that outside forces prevent you from being successful. Maybe you get ill, maybe you accidentally follow the wrong program, maybe it turns out you have a bad metabolism!

Finally, the goal is too far in the future. If your goal is to lose weight by next year, that then essentially gives you a license to procrastinate. The target is so far away, that you indulge yourself in a little overeating or put off exercise for a while and not worry about it until next month.

6 months pass and you realize you're actually _further_ from your goal.

And because it's too late, you're likely to just give up at this point.

Not a good goal!

What Good Goals Look Like

So, what does a good goal look like? How might you phrase this same objective in a manner that will increase your chances of success? The first thing to do, is to focus on things that are immediately within your control and that are not influenced by outside factors at all.

These goals should be things that you can accomplish in a guaranteed manner and that you will be immediately graded on a pass-fail basis.

So for instance, instead of aiming to lose some few kilos by next year, you would use this goal:

"I will work out three times a week, every week, for at least 15 minutes"

Now *that* is a goal that you can aim for. Regardless of your metabolism, or of injury, or of any other outside factor, this is a goal that you can accomplish. It also means you can't 'put off' the goal and it means you'll never reach that disappointing point where you can no longer stand any chance of completing it.

At any point in your life, there is no reason that you can't set out to accomplish this goal and expect to be successful.

But by focussing on this small *short term* goal, you will then find that the long-term goal of losing the weight takes care of itself.

How to Formulate Your Goals

But that doesn't mean that any short-term goal that is binary in nature is going to cut it.

First of all, you need to know what you want and make sure that the goal you are setting for yourself is going to help you get there. You need your goals to be intrinsically motivating and that means that you have to feel truly passionate about them.

It's only be following a goal you really feel excited about, that you will find you have the energy and motivation to keep going.

Working out for 15 minutes a day is an effective goal because it is sure to take you closer to your broader goal of losing weight. By keeping that end goal in mind, you should stand a better chance of staying motivated to work out even when you're feeling tired, or when you're feeling low on willpower.

And you shouldn't just be aiming to 'lose weight' either. Instead, you should have a more concrete vision of what this entails. Do you want to be thinner? Do you want to be more muscular? Why do you want that thing? Is it so that you will be more attractive to the opposite sex?

Or because you want more energy? Be honest with yourself and listen to that drive inside that is pushing you toward the goal you want to accomplish.

If your goal is to make money, then try to focus on what the emotional hook is that is making you want that money. It likely boils down to more than cash – maybe its status you really want? Power? Confidence? Freedom? Only by really understanding the true nature of your own dreams can you a) take the fastest route to accomplishing them and b) maintain the drive and motivation you're going to need to get there.

This is going to require some soul-searching!

Moreover, you need to ensure that the goals are achievable and realistic and that you have broken them down into small enough steps. Case in point: our goal for weight loss is to work out 15 minutes per day.

That's a tiny amount but it works because it's achievable and realistic. If you make your goal harder – such as working out for an hour a day – then you're going to find you're quickly disappointed when you can't find the time or the energy. You'll put off the exercise and make excuses.

The best part about training for just 15 minutes is that once you *start*, you'll often find you go for longer. Put it this way: it's much better to have a small, easy-to-accomplish goal and *stick with it*, than it is to have a massive, life-changing goal that you can't manage!

But of course if you're making your goal smaller, that means that it will take you longer to reach the eventual destination you're gunning for. This is not a problem: this is just another thing you need to accept if you want to accomplish anything. Things worth having-*take time*. Take small steady steps and enjoy the journey.

Time can be Converted or Transformed.

What is time anyway?? Why is it important so much?

Well you've heard people say that time is money, right? Well I say time is like energy. It cannot be created or regained, much like energy it can only be transformed, conserved and measured

Time is transformed whenever it is used to create or achieve something, for example, when you work at a nine to five job you get paid an hour, right?

Yes then when you add more time in your shifts, let's say you earn R15 (ZA) an hour and you work from 8am to 5pm, you will earn R135 (ZA) from the whole nine hours you worked.

This means you have transformed/converted time into money.

You've made nine hours of your life to become R135 (ZA) by simply spending your time at work hence the term "Time is Money".

But always beware that time can also be converted to anything negative like spending your time listening to or watching radio and TV programs that won't be worth your while.

Leading or can I say programing you to be ignorant, arrogant, filled with meaningless pride and very poor, most of all, unhappy.

On the Brightside, always look on the Brightside of things, all this energy, power or force of nature is within your control.

Imagine yourself being able to control and convert time to be anything you want and desire.

What would you do with it??

Well I would advise you to use this force of nature wisely and with caution. Use it to learn how to do the things you love, then use it again to achieve them.

Meet people you love, use it for giving, putting a smile on other people's faces, bring joy at home, wherever you may be, whatever you are doing, transform/convert time to your benefit and not your downfall.

You only have a few years to live, don't you want to fully enjoy those years??

Use the sharp mind that the Creator has given you to learn how to manage and properly convert your time.

Remember the conversion default of time is always negative, that's only when you take the initiative for it to be positive and that's why it's always hard to change and start over.

So act now and act today.

Time can be conserved.

Conserving time can be one of the hardest tasks a human can ever do. To conserve time you need to be more disciplined.

And discipline is one of the painful part of correction and we all hate it, right??

Wrong.

Discipline is the core and the most valuable phase one can undergo. It is not pleasant or easy to withstand, it is very painful and some would say hell.

But it helps us in a long run. Trust me we are all here to invest in long term success. Discipline teaches us that pain speaks and prevents our bad behaviour when we carefully listen to it and learn from it.

On the other side of pain there is always everlasting joy, immeasurable peace and love.

It will take time for you to learn from pain because during this phase of struggle in your life you will be more focused on pain and how you can't take it anymore.

I know it's hard but if you just listen and figure out why you in pain in the first place, that's where the solution lies. Pain will humble you and teach you save to time and use it sparingly.

Listen to Pain.

Time is measured by created moments

The whole point of time is to measure lifespans of living beings, evolutions and the world's existence.

But people like you and me should look a time differently.

How?

We should manage it, value it and put it into good use. The most prominent thing you can do with your time is to value it so much that you put it in good use all the time.

You should learn to use your time to do the things you love and these things should bring income in your pocket. That's the whole point isn't it? More money in and less money out.

Find ways to use your creativity to help you create wealth and the life you desire. Use it to learn new things, don't use it to pass time with movies, watching television programmes that don't help you or benefit you in anyway.

Time is valuable.

Everything else can be renewed, redone and rewritten like history but time can never go back.

Moments cannot be relived and we cannot rewind our youth. So do not save to do what makes you happy for later, do what you love now while you still young and capable.

You might have heard of the term "the future is in your hands" a lot, right??

Well, it's true, believe it and start creating now while you still got this precious gift we call time. Create moments and live in them with enjoyment, after all you only live once a day.

Learn time management today, your life depends on it.

This is it. It's Time to Move today.

"Don't gain the world and lose your soul;

Wisdom is better than silver and gold."

--

BOB MARLEY

CHAPTER 2

Study all the number ones in your field of choice.

Every field has people at the top. I'm talking about people who dominate in their respective fields of work and talent, people like for example:

- Rafael Nadal in tennis,
- Tiger Woods in golf,
- Bill Gates in Programming and
- Jeff Bezos in Ecommerce.
- Love him or hate him Donald Trump in the real estate industry.

I have to stop somewhere because the list is so long it can take me the whole day, in this case, the whole page to state every big shot there is in the whole world.

Learn from the best in your field.

Every person alive has a specific idea or preference of who he/she wants to be in life.

Believe it or not, in this day and age there is a big-shot in that niche/field of work. You must always prepare yourself to be the best every time and remember to seek help as well.

To love something is great, to be good at it is another. You have to improve the necessary skills required to harness your dream, if you don't have the skills required to be the best in your field of choice.

Now the only thing that will help you in this case is to get rid of your ego, pride and self-importance and put your gear on and start your journey to learn from the best.

Read their books, subscribe to their services, listen to their motivational speeches, and study what they did to get to the point they are at and even pass them, go to seminars most of all study their mistakes and remember to make your own mistakes as well.

Why studying their mistakes is so important and why is this the golden task??

The golden task

This is where the gold is my friend. When you study and analyse other people's mistakes so good that you even find the root cause of it.

Will be the most helpful and prominent way you can ever imagine and do.

What's the most amazing thing about this is that all these mistakes won't be repeated by you should you choose to take up the task yourself because you already know a lot about what not to do.

As they say "you can't fall in the same hole twice" isn't it?

Open your eyes to this victory secret for a moment. Imagine fixing all the mistakes of all the legends in your field of choice, you will pave a new way that has never been seen by mankind before.

What's also great about this is that you will create a new age of mistakes that will help others to succeed by simply fixing your own mistakes.

In other words you have the power to save the world by just fixing other people's mistakes and creating new ones that people can learn from.

And that, in my point of view, is success.

So what is success really??

Well throughout time some people have perceived success as a one-time event, an achievement or an award. This has time and time again been proven not to be true.

To me success is a mind blowing lifestyle.

A mind blowing lifestyle is a type of lifestyle where you win small fights in order to prepare yourself for the main event, the big fight that will change your situation for the better.

What I really mean is that you need to look at some of your favourite actors, most of them are made by a hit movie where their performance in that particular movie was the ultimate best and they brought home the academy award.

This goes the same with musicians "the one hit wanders", you know the ones I'm talking about right?

The same rules apply to success as well. I mean if you win once you will start to have a solid self-confidence and you will create a pattern of winning which will come automatically.

You will be classified with winners and this will create a positive reputation for you which will bring more success in your bosom, and not forgetting both powerful and influential friends that will help you on your journey.

Fame and fortune will follow. Good examples of this are Dwayne "The Rock" Johnson and J.K Rowling and you after you read and apply the advice of this manuscript.

The Formula – How to Structure Goals and Make Your Plan

Now you know the basis of what makes a great goal, it's time to actually start building these kinds of goals for yourself. In this chapter, we'll lay out some simple instructions that you can follow to begin putting these ideas into practice.

Later we'll be applying this same formula to different areas of your life, so that you can start going after a better body, better salary and better love life. But in each instance, we'll be reapplying this same strategy.

Step 1: Visualization

The first and most important step is to visualize what you want and to really *understand* what you want. We already discussed this a little in respect to becoming richer. Often you'll find it's not really the money that you want but rather what that money *represents* in terms of your lifestyle or your status.

The same goes for being fit. It's not enough to want to be thinner or healthier, you need to understand your own motivations for wanting that. Do you want to feel more physically capable, perhaps become a professional athlete? Do you want to prevent the deterioration that many experience as they age? Or do you want to look amazing so that you can be more successful with the opposite sex.

The best way to get an idea of what you want from life in any given area is often to just visualize your future. That means closing your eyes and just calling to mind your ideal future. Where are you? What do you look like? What do you do for a living? Who are you with?

By picturing your future in this abstract way, you'll be able to start analysing what it is that you're actually trying to accomplish and from there you can begin to look at the more concrete steps you'd need to take in order to get there.

Some other strategies that can help with this are:

- Looking at your role models and seeing what they have in common

- Thinking about the things that excite you, your hobbies, the things you're a fan of, etc.

- Thinking about the last time you felt truly happy, or truly alive

From there, it's also a good idea to think about the actual reality and to visualize what it would be like to get there and to live that life. Do you still want it?

For example, it's very easy to want to be a rock star in theory but you might not like the actual lifestyle: it would mean spending a lot of your life touring, being in the public eye and probably struggling to raise a family.

This is why we're thinking in abstractions at this point. Because you may find that the reality of being a rock star is not something you really want – in which case you're going to start again and tap into what it was about that lifestyle that appealed to you.

Are there other ways you can satisfy the same emotional goals? If you want to be recognized for your music, then you could try playing an instrument on YouTube or Band Camp! If you just want to be a professional musician, then you could compose music for computer games or videos.

But it doesn't all have to be about your career either: you could just as easily find that you're happy just busking, or making music in your spare time.

Getting to the core of what you want like this can also help you to overcome impossible odds. If you want to be an astronaut for example, then you might have to come to terms with the fact that you are too old and it's now unlikely to ever happen. But ask yourself *why* that appeals to you on an emotional level.

Maybe it comes down to your love of space, in which case you might be equally satisfied by being an astronomer? Maybe it comes down to your love of exploration and discovery, in which case you could be an explorer, or maybe just a researcher.

Step 2: Assess Your Situation Honestly and Thoroughly

The next crucial step is to assess your current position versus the ideal one that you have visualized. This is where you're going to analyse the gulf between real life and your dream future and then try and find what the best way to *bridge* that gulf is.

Making an honest appraisal of your current situation is a very important way to assess your current position and to thereby to get an idea of your strengths and weaknesses.

And in particular, you need to think about what advantages you have, what networks, what contacts and what opportunities. You may feel that you have none but that probably means you just haven't been through enough. As the saying goes: there's no such thing as a lack of resources, only a lack of resourcefulness.

This is also where you're going to analyse just how likely your goals are and then perhaps re-phrase them on that basis. If you've seen that you aren't likely to become an astronaut, then it's time to create a more achievable goal such as becoming an astronomer.

If your goal is to date incredibly hot women, then perhaps it's time to reassess and at least *start out* by aiming for women that are on a similar level to yourself.

Your mantra for this step is to assess your situation honestly and then take the 'path of least resistance'.

You're looking at the maximum benefit from the minimum time and work.

Step 3: Formulate a Plan

This brings us to the next step, which is to formulate a plan on the basis of your current situation, where you want to be and what options you have available to you.

For losing weight or getting into shape, this means looking – for example – at the different training programs. However, by making the honest assessment of yourself and your situation in the last step, you should be in a better position to choose a system that appeals to your particular strengths and weaknesses and that you are actually likely to see through.

So many people will pay for expensive training programs that involve eating a very strict diet and working out 10 times a week for an hour each session. But is that really realistic? If you've tried to stick at previous workouts and have failed, then the answer is *probably not.*

When you assess your current situation that also means assessing where things when wrong in the past and what your lifestyle and personality will allow for.

And by knowing this, you can then look for a training program or devise one that will work to *your* advantage. Maybe that means finding a way to fit CV in around your regular routine, or maybe it means sticking to a diet that you will find enjoyable and convenient.

The same goes for plans for travel and for your career. It's time to get real and to get your head out of the clouds. Stop dreaming about travelling the world and instead, think about how you're going to travel more despite your personal responsibilities, budgetary limitations etc. Stop wishing you were rich and start thinking about how you're going to climb the ladder in your career to actually get there.

When making your plan, it's also important to think outside the box and to reject the generally accepted beliefs regarding what you need to do to accomplish each goal.

(a) *Reject the Norm*

Because we are only really taught one way to get what we want and that is to progress through our careers. And this is why so many of us get stuck. We decide we want to be rich and so we work harder, instead of realizing that we could be wealthier on our current salaries by spending less and perhaps finding a secondary income. We think the only way to become successful in music is to keep working our day job to pay for it. We think that the only way to travel more is to work harder and then retire early.

But the costs of living will inevitably go up to meet your salary, you will have less and less time as you work harder and harder and take on more responsibility and you'll find there's never 'a good time' to accomplish your goals.

And so instead you need to take the path less travelled. There are other ways to getting to where you want to be and if you're just banging your head against the wall, then it's time to rethink that strategy.

There's nothing stopping you from starting a business in your spare time *right now*. There's no reason you can't quit your job and start travelling *tomorrow*. You have the abilities you need to begin applying for higher-paid jobs. What's holding you back?

Step 4: Phrase Your Goals in Small Steps

Now you know what it is you want to achieve and how it is you want to get there, you're going to hone in. You now know the 'bigger picture' and it's time to think about the small details instead.

You know you want to get fit, you know that going to the gym is not viable for you and you know that working out from home makes a lot more sense.

So all that's left to do is to phrase this as a goal that you can focus on every day or week. Hence:

"I will work out for at least 15 minutes every day"

Maybe you've decided you're not so interested in toning muscle but want to start by focussing on losing weight so you'll look better in a suit and feel more energetic. In that case, your goal might be:

"I will walk to and from work every day that it isn't raining"

There's nothing wrong with having more than one goal, or making more detailed goals either. You might couple this with a secondary goal, which could be:

"I will not eat anything on my 'foods to avoid list'"

Focus on these small steps and get yourself closer to your goal one bit at a time.

Likewise, if you want to advance your career, then your goal might be to:

"Take every opportunity that arises to enhance my CV"

Or

"Apply for one job in the evening, three times a week"

Some of your broader goals are going to take multiple steps. For instance, if your goal is to become a famous musician, then perhaps you should take the following steps:

- Learn to play the guitar by spending half an hour each evening, four days a week

- Save $15 a day to invest in studio equipment

- Output 1 video a week to build an audience

- Output 2 videos a week to build an audience

- Continue to output 2 videos a week and spend 1 hour per week in self-promotion activities

- Spend 2 hours a week working on an album to sell from the channel

It's a long process but it's also a *real strategy*. It's a strategy that you need to succeed. It represents a cognitive shift where you're no longer daydreaming about being a famous rock star and you're instead looking at concrete, realistic, achievable steps.

And that's when you start making real, actual progress!

"Great events do not come to pass overnight."

–

NAPOLEON HILL

CHAPTER 3

Improve your Speech.

Imagine yourself being the best at something or having created an art masterpiece for instance and you are at the very top, no one can even match you at this point because you're busy breaking your own records.

Let's use art for this illustration because I'm very fond of it. I love art to save my life.

Well enough about me, let's get back to the illustration. Now imagine you are this huge art sensation like the late great Pablo Picasso and you just created the never seen before art masterpiece.

You even getting invited talk about it at large art seminars, television show interviews, newspapers, radio shows, YouTube and the like, you know what I'm talking about.

Then the horror rises upon you like a sand-storm, you find yourself being unable to express yourself with picture painting words, yes, exactly like you do with your hands.

You're the best but you have stage fright and shy.

This will not just kill your vibe, without proper personality tools you will not be able to achieve greatness and form successful and beneficial relationships with your fans.

That will cause you to lose big time against your completion because people always, not all the time though, follow the most charismatic leader in the room, e.g. Nelson Mandela.

This is definitely the reason why you should include improving your speech as one of the main goal in your "things to improve" list.

Make it your main priority, your mission to achieve this phenomenon and be effective with it.

Paint pictures with your words.

So to paint a picture with words creativity and intrigue is required.

You don't have to go straight to the point, you need to create some sort of journey that raises or leads to the point you want to make.

Using words like the one I used at the beginning of this chapter ("imagine" is the key word here).

Start with words like "how it began, imagine, this reminds me of, etc." before you render a relevant illustration that will help you to perfectly paint a relevant picture in the listeners' minds.

Remember you always have to commit yourself to improving your speech and how you interact with others, for this is very critical and important.

Learn how to ask informative questions.

Asking informative questions will help you find out about things you never knew or learn some ideology you've never knew before.

But always this keep in mind that not all knowledge is useful or worth finding.

You just have to figure out what you really want to achieve in your life and be firm on that decision then pursue the knowledge and necessary skills required to achieve it.

Because all this will use up your time and maybe you could be after it half of your life.

The worst case scenario might be that you get it and cease where at that position in life or even die trying to achieve it.

Do not chase great moments or good feelings because they change all the time.

What I'm really trying to say here is that do not spent most of your energy to live in a single moment of your dreams, use it to create a person of your dreams out of your current self.

Send most of your energy defeating and challenging your negative or rather self-defeating mental beliefs that you have where your self-image is concerned.

Always dream and act as a winner. Do not even think about winning moments because a moment according to me is a point in time that uses up your emotion, time and energy, it is stored in your sub-conscious memory as a point of reference of how you feeling at that particular time.

Moment affect you whether good or bad, they are so relevant in human evolution that when they are built up or joined from the time of your birth and the time you die, they sum up as your whole story in your lifetime.

And in them we find your victories and defeats and they also determine to the next generation as a hero or just ordinary.

What is most important is that they determine the type of person you are and who you've grown to be. Don't chase moments, create them.

Your words have immeasurable power.

How would you feel if I said to you right now, that all of your words create or stop situations from happening and that you have all the control of this amazing power?

It feels good to be a superhero for a change, isn't it?

Well you might not be super-strong as superman/superwoman or as smart as iron man but you definitely are the superhero of your life and you can use your words to change your situation.

Before I get deep on the how, I want to touch on something very important and you probably noticed it as you go along reading this book.

I did not in any way shown you how to apply these principles that I teach you in the previous chapters because I am giving you an opportunity to take the first step and open up your imagination.

What I am trying to say here is that, I want you to create your own illustrations by applying the principles in your life.

I want you to act now, today!

Now as I was saying before the heartfelt speech I just did.

Your words have power especially you say them out loud and believe them they will happen.

How so?!

Well look at the people who have strong opinions about everything, and I mean everything. They have a strong belief that they are either smart or always right, this is a great believe to have only if you either self-centred or I'm sorry to say this dumb.

None, not even a single person in this world knows everything because we all know in part in all general knowledge available to us.

So as much as I like to encourage you to make bold statements about yourself. I urge you not to do this when you don't have the knowledge, the tools and skills required to prove that statement to be true.

First find the knowledge, get the tools required and a master the skill then make a bold claim that you're the best.

Choose statement and your words wisely.

Choose and use your words wisely. Other than saying "I can't do it" say "I can't do it, yet", did you see what I just did right there?

I opened up a world of infinite possibilities by just adding the word that kills all negativity and opens up a door for learning.

If you've been with me since the beginning of this chapter, you will come to a realisation that simply by the correct use of your words you can reignite the desire or drive to make a change in your situation and reap pleasant benefits in the foreseeable future.

By simply improving your speech, you just erased all possible negative future limitations in your life. You will experience tremendous peace and self-love that is unimaginable.

Letting Go of Fear

I'm going to be honest with you now: there's a chance that you already know this deep down.

It makes logical sense that you should be making small, concrete steps to achieve your goals rather than making bombastic plans to 'become a rock star' or abstract visions like 'get richer'.

So what has been preventing you from doing that?

Two things:

1. <u>It's a lot of work</u> – it's much easier and more satisfying to dream big and get the reward that comes from that, rather than face the reality of grinding towards your goals. We'll be discussing this more in this book later on, when we discuss how to stay motivated and stick to your goals even when the going gets tough. Then there's the matter of feeling like it's not the right time: you procrastinate instead of looking for other work. Again, this just needs a bit of rocket fuel, which we'll be looking at later on as well.

2. <u>You're afraid</u>. This is what I see so often and it's what condemns so many of us to a dull and unexciting lifestyle. We just don't want to take that leap and put ourselves out there. And in fact, it's easier to imagine ourselves as being very successful and to pretend we're going to get around to it, than it is to put ourselves out there and risk having our ego shattered when things don't go our way.

We're about to address that second issue. Because if you want to be successful, then it's no good to continue procrastinating or trying to put off taking that plunge!

How to know if you're Procrastinating?

Some examples of procrastinating include:

*   <u>Spending ages reading books and researching the topic instead of just getting stuck in</u>. I see this a ton when it comes to fitness goals. So many people will spend countless hours reading books and blogs on fitness programs, hiring consultants and buying gym kits. But the one thing they never do? Actually start working out! There's nothing wrong with researching health and fitness of course. In fact, it should be applauded. The problem is when you use this as a convenient excuse for not actually

32

training. The reality is that *any* training program is better than nothing. If you want to start getting into shape – if you really stand *any chance* of success – then you should start doing press ups and pull ups right now. There is simply no reason not to. You can then improve your routine over time but you start NOW.

• <u>Working on projects and never completing them</u>. I work as an app developer and have released two highly successful apps in my lifetime that have together earned me in the region of $90,000. Not life-changing amounts over the course of a few years but certainly enough to make my life a little more comfortable, especially as they continue to earn money while I work my regular job. As a result of this, I am often approached by people who tell me that they're planning on releasing a successful app too. They then work on it for three years and never release it. The difference between them and me? I released my app when it was an MVP – minimum viable product. This is called the 'fail fast approach' and we'll talk about it more as we go on. Point is though, I put myself out there whereas they made excuses. Perfectionism is often just a delay tactic. Assess yourself!

• <u>Claiming the time isn't right</u>. We touched on this briefly but just to recap: the time is *never* right. You're not travelling now because money isn't good? Sure, save up some cash – but by then you'll probably be at an exciting point in your career and not want to take a break. Then you'll have a partner and not want to leave them. Then you'll have a kid. There is never a good time to start a relationship, to get married, to have kids, to travel, to start a business. You do it anyway. And if you're worried what other people might say? Then follow the advice to 'ask for forgiveness, not permission'. Do it and worry about the consequences later. If it really means that much to you, then it is really the only option you have.

• <u>Ignoring your own dissatisfaction</u>. Do you know anyone in your life who clearly wants to be in a relationship and who ignores this fact by throwing themselves into their career? Every post on social media is about how excited they are about their new job, or about their travel. But you suspect that really, they just wish they had someone to go home to? In this case, they are trying to cover up one lacking area in their lives by focussing on the other. What about people who claim they are happy without pursuing their dream career because they have a family? Sure, that's great… but why not go for both? And that way be able to inspire your children with your inspiring story? Don't make this mistake because you need to be fulfilled in *every* area of your life if you're going to be truly happy.

Fear Setting

If you still can't overcome these psychological blocks though, then it time to employ a technique known as 'fear setting' that was described by Tim Ferris in his book: *The Four Hour Workweek*.

The idea here is simple: you are going to write down all of the things holding you back and all of the things you're afraid of and then you're going to present counterarguments, contingency plans and more to *remove* those fears.

So take a moment to think about your goals and dreams and then write down all of the things that you want to accomplish. Write those goals and the steps you need to take as we discussed in the last chapter and then think about taking that first step right now. What's holding you back? What are your fears? Be honest and thorough and make sure to include every possible concern.

Let's say you want to start your own business. Here are your fears and concerns:

- You don't have the money
- Taking out a loan may be reckless and leave you in serious debt if the business isn't a success
- Your partner might see your investment as irresponsible and lead to relationship problems
- You might lose your job and find yourself without stable income
- You might be unable to find future work and that could lead to your family going hungry and you losing your home
- Your business might be a failure and make you look like a failure too

Now go through each of these objections and address how likely they really are and how you can deal with them/prevent them.

For example:

- You don't have the money and
- Taking out a loan may be reckless and leave you in serious debt if the business isn't a success. Consider a PayPal loan, this is a loan that you pay back only through PayPal income, meaning, that you won't owe anything until you start earning or:
    - Try Kick-starter
    - Bootstrap your business – design it in a way that will allow you to start the business for less
    - Consider asking parents for a business loan
    - Look for a business partner with capital to invest
- Your partner might see your investment as irresponsible and lead to relationship problems. Your partner is more likely to support you in your ambitions:
    - If you use the above methods, you can demonstrate that you have been sensible and taken every precaution
    - You can even take out business insurance
    - Your partner might even be able to help you bring in extra income to support your goals
    - Have a rainy day fund
    - Explain to them the risks and why it's important to you
- You might lose your job and find yourself without stable income and you might be unable to find future work and that could lead to your family going hungry and you losing your home.
- In most cases, you'll find that your employer will offer you your job back if you need it
    - At the very least, you can probably find lower-level work to fund your survival, even if that means just doing a part-time job.
    - You don't have to quit your day job until you've proven to yourself that you can make money from your business idea or even maintain a part-time salary in the meantime.
    - You can probably survive on a lower salary than you think and for longer than you think.

- Your business might be a failure and make you look like a failure too, so you will do market research and take every precaution to ensure your plan is a success and you will gain advice from knowledgeable third parties. Who cares what other people think right.

The alternative is never trying to make anything of yourself or pursue your passions which is far worse. Okay and with that out the way, now we can start actually making progress in the various areas of your life that you want to improve!

"I will allow no person's opinion, no influence to enter my mind which does not harmonise with my purpose."

–

MANUEL L. QUEZON

CHAPTER 4

Be practical and keep up with the times.

Well by this time you have heard a lot of speeches and learned a lot of things, by doing this, you now have a burning desire of achieving major success.

The top question you should ask yourself is that are you applying the knowledge?

Are you doing whatever it takes to achieve what you want to achieve or do you still face the same situation hoping to get a different results?

If that's so stop procrastinating and be do the work. I want you to focus and stay the course.

Take unlimited action!

Be Practical.

One of the reasons I do not show you practical examples In this book is because I want you to be creative and take unlimited action on whatever task you have at hand, and see to it that you finish it whether it's difficult or not.

I want you to be practical, meaning that I want you to learn something today and do it right away.

Making this your new habit will help you a lot because as they say "practice makes perfect." So in that context you will be able to be good at something because you do it every day.

It's like running. Remember when you first learned to walk? You can't because it's so easy now that you can do it with your eyes closed and you were a mere toddler when you first learned it.

You can't remember it, but the trick here is you did not forget it.

Why? You might be asking yourself.

Well the answer is; everything you do is recorded in your mind and it becomes habitual when you do it often, that's when it's recorded in your subconscious mind and that task becomes automatic.

Be careful of which task you make automatic in your life.

You know in life sometimes we make poor and good choices and they can both be beneficial or they can easily destroy our lives.

For this reason you must always stay alert of your own decisions good or bad. They might be the end or the beginning of a great time in your life.

So how do you know your decision is a good/bad one??

Based on my experience I detect a bad choice when let's say I have or I'm in a difficult situation and I can't get out of it and I have a list of choices/decisions to make.

Like for instance, choosing between being a thief and going to find a pride crushing job just to provide some basic needs for yourself and family.

In this case being a thief is the easy way out and finding a job will take a longer period of time to even smell the life of your dreams.

Because the longer way requires you to change your habits first, seek knowledge, open up yourself to learning, learning how to overcome defeat, and do all the hard work that comes with it.

While being a thief is only the opposite, the easy way out.

Open up to learning new habits that align you to win and succeed.

At first they will be conflicts between doing what you used to do and what you want to do now, because your subconscious will be in the process of rebooting, deleting the old habits and replacing them with the new ones.

After sometime your habits will change when you do the acts every day, they will become automatic and that's when you start to notice drastic changes in your personality, belief system, reasoning and relationships.

You will start to get more wins than loses, old friends that had no purpose will leave you, your lifestyle and money management will change.

Your whole life will change. You will become unrecognisable to family, friends, and colleagues. Most importantly you will be unrecognisable to yourself.

Choose the good habits to be automatic. It might be challenging but you can do it.

I believe in you.

Keep up with the times.

As much as I know how challenging it could be when it comes to learning a new subject, stunt, strategy or how to something for the first time.

It will require you to eliminate all your defeating self-image beliefs and do all the required back end work.

The back-end work is the work required before doing the actual work.

You can call it practicing the newly acquired skill, reading the how to book before investing, you get the point, don't you?

 So you need to always be ready to do the back-end work, for its like getting through hell for heavenly results in the end.

The world is changing in a fast pace like never before so be ready to change with it, also learn to study more quickly and effectively.

Have a clear picture of your dream in mind.

Here's an awesome trick, if you going through tough times right now and you need something to hold on to and strong enough to hold you, prevent you from falling apart.

You need to have a clear picture of for your desires in mind, visualise the in detail know even how they will come about in your life and which path to take.

When your dream virtualisation is strong, your faith and hope will increase exponentially.

You will experience contentment and above all peace that you've never imagined before.

When challenges come you'll know exactly what to do, who to call and you will find good references to numb the pain you feeling at that particular moment.

Your spirit will be strong because you have a solid point of reference as to why you do what you do.

Your journey will be an amazing experience. For if you clearly know your **"why"**, you will then begin to your **"when"** then ultimately your **"how"**.

As this process is happening, you will discover that anything is acquirable and it all can be learned as long as you willing to put up the work required.

Virtualise the path, the work and the end results for this will be the blueprint to not only your success, but your happiness and peace.

All that is required of you is to be brave and fight.

How to Make Your Fitness Goals Happen

We've seen the basics of how to accomplish your general goals, now it's time to accomplish *specific* goals. For this chapter, we're going to look at fitness and how you're going to apply the principles we've discussed to getting into awesome shape.

So the first thing you need to know is why you want to improve your fitness and what you want that to really look and feel like. Is your goal to get fitter so you can play sports again? Do you want to look awesome for your own satisfaction? Do you want to be powerful so that you feel more physically intimidating? Do you want to be healthier? Or maybe attract members of the opposite sex?

And what is your current situation? What have you tried in the past? Why has it not worked? What is your current shape and size? What are your physical strengths and best attributes? What do you enjoy doing? How much time do you have?

This is all very important because it is going to drastically change the way you go about accomplishing your objectives.

For example, if you are a man and your goal is to be more physically intimidating, then you might decide that it makes the most sense to bulk. This means adding the most mass possible in the shortest amount of time, in order to become a tank. It involves eating a ton of calories and even more protein, resting a lot and lifting heavy weights.

On the other hand, if you want to become toned and lean to attract women, then you are going to want to eat less and get more aerobic exercise such as walking, running, skipping etc.

You also need to think about the exercise that you enjoy doing, the exercise that is practical to work into your routine, any physical limitations such as illnesses or joint problems etc.

How to Set and Stick to Realistic Goals

One of the most important considerations when coming up with a training program, is making it fit into your routine. Think about when you have free time, how your energy levels are at different points during the day and what you can do to capitalize on the moments in your routine that are free for training.

Step 1 - Fitting it in.

One of the best ways to lose weight for example is to walk more. Walking is ideal because it burns a good number of calories without exhausting you, or making you sweaty. That means you can conveniently fit it into your routine and do it regularly without it becoming unfeasible.

And most of us can easily fit more walking into our routine. For example, you might find that you can use your lunch break at work to go on a long walk. If you have 60 minutes at lunch, you can eat for 10 minutes and spend the other 50 walking (it's best to walk at the *end* of the 60 minutes).

A 50 minute walk each day should easily be enough to hit your 10,000 step goal, which is around 8 kilometres and should lead to an additional 3,000 calories (roughly) burned each week. That's the amount of calories you normally burn in a day. More importantly it will build your fitness significantly, give you more sunlight and fresh air.

So forget trying to do intense HIIT workouts 5 times a week that leave you exhausted... just go for a nice walk that will conveniently fit into your routine!

Likewise, you can fit a walk in by getting off the bus early, by walking home from work etc.

The same goes for diet. My advice is to stick to a rigid diet *only* in the morning and at lunch. Why? Because most of us will want to make our evenings a time to enjoy a fun meal with our partners. Or we want to go out with friends and enjoy pudding.

Conversely, breakfast and lunch tend to be more functional – eaten alone and in a hurry. That means you can much more easily reduce your calories or your carbs at this time during the day and then 'cut lose' in the evening.

Think about ways you can make this more convenient for you too. If you pass a shop that sells protein shakes in bottles each morning, then maybe switch your morning coffee for a morning protein shake. This is ideal if you find that the thought of mixing your protein shake and getting it all over the floor potentially is putting you off of actually eating it!

Another example might be to work out from home if you are struggling to get to a gym, or to take up swimming if there just so happens to be a pool next to your office.

Step 2 - Enjoy It

Your exercise should be something you enjoy. If you have tried and failed to build lean muscle with weights, then clearly you're not cut out for it. Apparently it just doesn't appeal to what you enjoy.

But all of us should find there's *some* form of exercise we enjoy. Maybe you should get yourself a pair of parallel bars (which are very cheap) and take up gymnastics or hand-balancing at home?

Or instead, how about taking up rock climbing. Rock climbing is *fantastic* for building big, powerful muscle, particularly in the lats and forearms. Maybe you'll find that you love boxing: getting yourself a heavy bag is a great, enjoyable way to build big shoulders in particular. Or maybe you might be cut out for power lifting?

Whatever the case, find a form of training. This is what all the most powerful people with the most incredible physiques have in common. They don't just love being big, they love *getting* big. They eat, sleep and dream the gym and they love everything from the feeling of the chalk on their hands, to hanging out with other swole people.

You need to discover that passion not just for the end destination but for the journey to get there.

Step 3 - Play to Your Strengths

Some people are ectomorphs naturally, some are endomorphs. This determines whether you're a big, bulky type or a lean 'hard gainer'.

Where possible, try to align your goals to your natural strengths (remember step 2?). So for example, if you are an endomorph, then you can focus on becoming a massively powerful hulk. If you're an ectomorph, then why not go for the lean look that a lot of people love?

There's nothing wrong with chasing after the harder dream of course but if you're flexible, shoot for the one that you're already gifted in. That way, the results will come faster and you'll find it more intrinsically rewarding, more quickly.

Another tip is to find role models that are similar to you. Look for people who started in your situation, people who have body types similar to your own, but who have made the very most of them.

Those are the people to listen to when it comes to training advice because they have worked with (most likely) a similar genetic starting point and similar set of circumstances in life to begin with.

Step 4 - <u>Take it Slow</u>

Remember what we said in the earlier chapters: a good goal for fitness should involve working out for 15 minutes, maybe even 10 minutes. Don't come up with insane strategies that involve training twice a day, or you'll find that you gain muscle quickly and lose it quickly.

Be willing to see small improvements over time so you don't burn out.

Conversely though, don't take it *so* slow as to not see results. The objective here is to use the MED – 'Minimum Effective Dose'. That means you're committing just enough time to actually see progress, so that you can start to assess and judge your strategy and so that you can improve it over time. Don't do more, don't do less.

***

By doing all of this, you should have come up with a training program that is effective for you specifically and for your lifestyle and genetics.

If you have tried and failed to take up weightlifting several times in the past, then maybe it's time that you took a different approach by swimming three times a week after work. Or by getting a heavy bag and punching that for 40 minutes a few times a week. Maybe you just do 15 minutes of press ups before bed.

Whatever the case, start doing something right away and then experiment to find what works for you.

"LOSERS AVOID FAILING AND
FAILURE TURNS LOSERS INTO WINNERS."

—

ROBERT T. KIYOSAKI

CHAPTER 5

Find a way always and not excuses

How to Make Your Career Goals Happen

Too many people have mistaken ideas when it comes to their approach to their careers. We often believe that working incredibly hard in jobs that we don't truly enjoy is 'responsible' and what adults should do. We often feel that we don't really have any choice when it comes to what we do for a living. We often feel scared to try anything else.

And this is why so many of us are unhappy in our careers: we just 'let them happen' and accept the career path that we fall into. We leave school or college, take the first job opportunity that comes out way, and then work hard to progress up the ladder. We never take a moment to actually ask: is this what I want? Do I have a choice?

Here are some ways to apply the principles that we've discussed to making progress in your career...

Knowing What You Want

The first and most important thing to focus on here is step 3 – coming up with your plan. It's time to acknowledge that you don't *have* to continue working a job you don't like and there's no reason that you even need to focus on your career at all.

The first myth we need to dispel then, is the notion that you need to get your sense of satisfaction and progress from your career at all. That is to say that you should be able to get the same satisfaction from a hobby.

We often feel that our sense of self-worth and achievement is tied up in our careers and that we need to work harder and harder in order to feel like we're progressing in life. But while you might be CEO of a logistics company, you are still ultimately in charge of making sure people get staplers – when your passion might be painting works of art.

This is why you can often do better to simply switch your focus to your 'extra curricula activities'. My sister did this as an artist when she realized that the reality of her intended field (creating props for movies) was not quite as idealistic as she had hoped.

So instead, she took on a job that would pay the bills by working as a saleswoman and then used her *spare time* to work on her creations in her own time.

She has gone on to receive quite a following on social media and has sold several of her works to private buyers. So although her career isn't something she gets particularly excited about, she still gets that sense of progress and excitement and doesn't *need* to keep taking on more responsibilities to feel happy and fulfilled.

And that also brings us to the other point: your wealth isn't entirely determined by your career either. You can just as easily augment your income through other means – whether that means renting out your room or whether it means cutting the neighbours' hair.

This is once again why it is important to consider the precise nature of your goals – if your goal is to be richer, then you can do it by shrinking expenses, by finding other sources of income etc.

If your goal is to get more status then you may be happy to progress in your current career. If it is to be fulfilled in your artist endeavours, or to be acknowledged for your ideas, then you may prefer to focus on working on projects outside the office.

This is essentially what we refer to as 'lifestyle design'. Lifestyle design means that you're focussing on what you can do to create your perfect lifestyle and you're looking for the path of least resistance to get there. This might not mean working more – it might mean working less and even taking on a 'menial' job, so that you can put more energy into other areas of your life.

Heck, it might mean creating income from elsewhere so that you can afford to work 4 days a week.

Why not!

Creating a Fool Proof Strategy

We've address the power that fear can have over us and the way it can prevent us from going after our goals. This is especially true when it comes to achieving things in our careers. And for that reason, it makes sense for us to take a look at some of the things we can do to make our career goals less risky.

For example, a lot of people will make the statement that they want to look for another job but that they can't because they have too many responsibilities. They might even make the unfounded claim that they wouldn't be able to find another that would pay the same salary... without looking!

But there is no reason that this needs to be seen as a risky undertaking and no reason that you should be afraid to look for work: the simple answer is just to look for other jobs while you are working your *current* job. Spend a couple of evenings looking at other jobs and applying for them and only leave your current job when you have a new one: zero risk.

The same goes for starting a part-time business. You don't have to immediately transition from one job to another when you can simply use your spare time in the evenings or in the weekends to work on your new business idea.

Only once you are certain it works should you then consider leaving your current job in order to take on the new one and this will present you with another risk-free way to transition to a job or career you love?

You can even try reducing your work hours and then use that extra free time in order to work on your business. Take a part time job and during your longer free hours, work on your business project.

The same goes for investment. If you need investment to create a business idea then there are lots of risk-free ways to get it. Using Kick-starter these days is a great option for example and involves zero risk as well as a great way to test the reception for your idea.

Likewise, you could ask your parents for investment, you could get a business partner friend, or you could take out a credit card loan. As long as you don't quit your current job, you can just make sure that the loan repayment terms are something you could manage to pay off if you had to and that way, you won't be putting yourself at any risk.

If you really want to make this happen, then you can always find a way.

And if you have assessed your vision and you just want to be a rock musician, then don't be distracted by trying to get rich. Focus to start with on doing the thing you love and finding more time for it. Let success come as a by-product.

As soon as you start working on your project, you'll find that it is rewarding and you now have a drive and passion that wakes you up in the morning and makes you more animated, more passionate and more exciting to be around for others even. It doesn't even *matter* if you are a success.

And that's why you should also view 'failure' simply as a chance to reassess your strategy and try something else. When you take this approach, there is really no way you can fail.

The Path of Least Resistance

Remember, genuinely going after something you want means taking the most direct and practical route to getting there: the path of least resistance. In this case, that means creating a business idea that you can realistically accomplish, or designing one around your current contacts and ideas.

One common mistake that a lot of people make is coming up with ideas they think will change the world. If that is your vision, then it doesn't also need to be a money making venture to begin with.

But if your vision (step 1) was to become wealthy, maybe to gain financial independence, then the most effective way to accomplish that goal is to focus on tried and tested methods for making money.

That is to say that you don't need to break the mould and come up with whole new business models. You don't need to become the next Mark Zuckerberg. Because there are billions of these huge projects that fail every year.

Meanwhile, just count the number of successful shops, clothes lines, resellers, building companies, hair dressers. There's nothing wrong with taking an idea that you've seen work and then just following it through to the letter. You now have a blueprint for success and you aren't having to reinvent the wheel.

Likewise, think about your resources and contacts. If you happen to know the editor of a gardening magazine, then that is an incredibly powerful contact to have and you should make the most of that – start a gardening service and use them to advertise!

You should also play to your strengths and if you know a lot about gardening, then once again, this is a good choice for your career. Very often, branching out (no pun intended) to start your own business will make most sense if you stick in your current industry: this way you'll have the expertise, experience and contacts to give yourself a great head-start.

Remember step 2: assessing your current situation and your resources. Make a list of everything you have available to you, all your skills, all your limitations and then think about what business and lifestyle changes will help you to get

The Fail Fast Model

Remember when we discussed how fear could hold some people back and one way this presented itself was when someone would work on perfecting their product without actually *releasing* anything? Not only is this a blatant delay tactic but it also means that if you eventually *do* release your product, you risk suffering a devastating defeat if it doesn't go to plan.

This happened to a friend of mine who had an idea for a business and then spent the next 3 years perfecting it. He trademarked the business name, took on a legal advisor, even paid for an expensive launch party! All for what essentially amounted to a website.

He tested the site in every browser and every display size *meticulously*, he conducted copious amounts of market research and he paid for tons of server space and bandwidth ready to cope with the inevitable huge amounts of traffic. But his upfront and ongoing costs were so high that he went bankrupt almost immediately.

The opposite approach is the 'fail fast model'. If you have an idea for a business, then you should create an MVP or 'minimal viable product'. This is the most basic, affordable and easy version of your product or service that you can release to the market immediately. That way, you can now test market response to it without having invested lots of your time and money into it.

You throw lots of ideas at the wall, quickly putting together something that works. If the idea is successful, you can then invest time and money into it. If it isn't, you iterate, learn from your mistakes and move on!

"BEAUTY IS NOT IN THE FACE;

BEAUTY IS A LIGHT IN THE HEART."

–

XPONENT WORLD

CHAPTER 6

How to Make Your Relationship Goals Happen

Relationships are something we often don't think of as 'goals' but they are in precisely the same way as any other. Maybe you're single and want to be in a relationship? Maybe you're in a relationship and want to make it better? Maybe you just want more success with the opposite sex? These are all worthwhile goals and all of them can be subjected to the precise same strategy that we looked at before.

Taking Stock

Here though, perhaps the most important aspect to look at is step 2: appraisal. You need to really take the time to assess the current state of your relationships and of yourself and then to work on moving forward and improving those areas of your life.

This starts by looking honestly at your current relationship. A lot of people will remain in unhappy relationships because they can't face admitting to themselves that things aren't perfect; perhaps because they have a child or house together, perhaps because they love their partner.

But note that improving your relationships doesn't necessarily have to mean ending your relationship. You can work on a relationship just like you can work on a car, or a business. You can improve the way the relationship works, improve your happiness in your role and generally see positive change over time.

Would you be happier if you had more sex? Are you getting enough time to spend with your partner properly? Do you argue more than you'd like? Sometimes, it is just a case of making some simple changes which can help you to improve on those areas and your relationship will be better for it. Don't live in denial.

Likewise, if you currently aren't having any success with approaching people, or if you're single and you don't want to be, then you maybe need to address certain aspects of your game in order to change how you are coming across.

This is a skill that can be learned like any other and often it comes down to appearing confident and presenting yourself well. If you can do that – without coming across as arrogant – then you will have much better luck approaching people.

Often people who never have any success in dating are portraying themselves in the wrong way. Maybe you're too shy to approach women/men and this means that you never get to choose who you date.

Maybe it's a confidence issue and you feel that you *can't* approach them without being rejected. Or perhaps you approach but you are coming across sleazy, awkward, or generally unattractive.

Creating a Plan for Dating

The aim is to look confident, successful and likeable. This sends a powerful and strong signal that others respond to as meaning that you're likely to be a great 'catch'. In other words, if you are projecting yourself as being very confident, then others will assume you have good *reason to be*.

This speaks to our evolutionary imperative: to go after people who are of a higher status than us, people who will provide good genetic material for our offspring, or people who have resources.

And this is where we can employ step 3: creating a 'fool-proof' and 'non-conventional' plan to achieve that. For example:

- Head to a bar with some friends, chat with them and have some drinks. Try to appear like a fun group to spend time with.

- While you're there scout out the room. Look for women/men who are within your reach. In other words, look for people who aren't *too* far out of your league. But don't be afraid to punch above your weight.

- If you see someone you like, shoot them a smile. If they are at all interested, they'll smile back.

- This *immediately* helps you to remove any risk of being rejected. If they're not interested, they won't look back and you'll just avert your attention elsewhere. If the person you spot is really keen, they might even take the initiative and head over!

- If not, you head over to them. Now crucially, don't focus in one the person you like but rather introduce yourself to the group and let your two groups mingle. This is your chance to demonstrate that you are fun, outgoing likeable and confident. You are displaying alpha male/female behaviour and making yourself the centre of attention. What's more, is that you're demonstrating that you are popular (as you have a group of friends) and that you get on with *their* friends. And what you're also doing, is showing that you might not be interested in them at all – which makes you much *more* desirable.

- If things go well, then you can offer the person you're interested in a drink. This sends a clear signal without saying as much and if they come with you, that's your chance to get them alone. If they said yes to the drink, then you can ask them to dance – again without losing face if they say no.

This plan relies on a couple more factors, all of which are within your control. You need a group of friends to help you for instance and you need the confidence to approach the group and to make yourself the centre of attention.

This takes practice and that can be your short term goal – practicing this technique until it comes as second nature and you really *do* feel confident and charming around members of the opposite sex.

Knowing What You Want

Again though, it is important to take into account step 1 here: knowing precisely what it is that you want. It is crucial that you are approaching the right type of partner and that you are sending the right signal.

It is a very different set of tools and approach that you need if you want to approach people for one night stands, versus approaching people that you want to have a long-term relationship with.

The former means going to bars and looking for people sending certain signals.

The latter might mean getting closer to a friend, or looking for someone who has a lot in common with you and who is *also* ready to settle down. If you want to play the field then you might consider using sites like Tinder.

"MONEY IS ONLY A TOOL.

IT WILL TAKE YOU WHERE YOU WISH,

BUT IT WILL NOT REPLACE YOU AS THE DRIVER."

—

THATO MOAHLODI

CHAPTER 7

The Power of Association.

In this interesting section of the book. I will start by saying, to associate is, according to the oxford dictionary, to connect things in your mind, spend time or have dealings with a group of people.

An illustration to this would be a person saying something like: "I don't associate Ryan with fitness and healthy living."

That would mean Ryan is a kind of guy that delights in a lot of junk food and forgets to exercise and eat his vegies.

So to initiate all the fire back in your motivated heart, I confidently say:

Do not associate the things you love with pain.

All the things you love will not be delightful when they are done out of a place of doubt, hard work and the 'I have to' mentality.

Let me further explain the above mentioned three scenarios.

Self-doubt is never worth it. It sprouts defeat.

I will start with doing what you love from a place of doubt. If you do what you love and maybe try to sell it or even doubt to approve it to someone if it's a manual whereby that particular person might learn a thing or two from it.

You'll never reap the rewards from it because the root cause of your self-doubt will spread to everything you do if you do not carefully rehabilitate your poor self-image.

No one will believe in your product if you do not believe in it yourself. No one will buy a product from you if you don't even believe what you're saying when you market it.

Hope by now you get my point. If not, I am saying that believe in yourself and all your abilities and you will ooze out positivity and success.

And if that happens, guess what? All people around you will start to buy your stuff and not only that, they will also recommend and believe in you.

You will start making those sales and you will also get that promotion you always wanted, and here is a cherry on top, you will have more wealth and believe that you only produce masterpieces from all your work.

The key phrase here is "doubt less, believe more."

This brings me to my second point.

Associating what you love with hard-work.

People like me, I am talking about people who love what they do here, do not exactly understand or find it impossible to believe the phrase "I did it and achieved it all through hard-work."

Because, I don't know if you're with me here, I believe hard-work is painful and makes everything unenjoyable as humanly possible.

I believe that if you do what you love you will not get tired from doing it and you will be motivated to do it and do it better.

You'll never, in any light of day, be woken up by some alarm clock.

You'll do it even if you're not getting paid from it, you'll love it and you will cherish it so bad that you go out and show everyone how you are the best at what you do and how it's a magnificent masterpiece.

I hope by sharing all that, I have really convinced you that when you do whatever it maybe that you love, to you will not feel like hard-work at all.

No matter how complicated it may be, you'll still believe it can be done.

No matter the cost and how much you get paid, you will still wake up early and do it with a smile and encouragement and finally understand the phrase "love conquers all".

Love what you do and it won't feel like work at all.

The third and final point in this matter.

Associating things you love with the "I have to" mentality.

Have you ever said word like "to make money or to get that promotion *I have to* do this or that"? I bet my African roots you did, because I have said it almost my whole life I even lost count along the way.

I did not understand at first that whenever I say this phrase (I have to) it birthed procrastination in my heart. I started wondering about the end results, which were all negative by the way, and nothing positive came about from anything I did at the time.

I learned to quit all that and look I wrote and finished a seven chaptered book you're reading right now in record time. Something I thought I would never do because I always felt like I have to.

So to get rid of the "I have to" mentality, like me. You must switch up the words with "I'd love to" mentality.

Try it and see what happens whenever you say "I'd love to do this or that".

I guarantee you that this kind of mentality will kill all the negative thought you had about whatever you want to do and guess what? It will eliminate procrastination.

Why? You might ask, what's the secret to this?

Well the secret is simple and yet again it all has to do with association.

Here is the secret, you'll probably laugh when you read this.

It's so simple and you used to do it as a child and now because you've all grown, you reverse engineered it by not focusing mainly on it.

You learned to focus on other non-beneficial stuff that ruins everything good and praiseworthy.

Like focusing on a relationship and associating it with happiness while happiness is not a relationship but a moment or focusing on music as a stress release for you.

While music is purely for your entertainment and it helps you to understand certain situations in your life and how to deal with them.

For what is worth learn to face what you're facing head-on and be brave enough to ask for help where needed.

Always know that whatever situation you might be facing right now somebody else might have faced a similar thing and he/she might teach you a thing or two on how to get things done and find the confidence to persevere.

Get rid of all the chains that are holding you back from success only you have the key to do that and the ball is always on your court.

Do not look at someone to do the task for you, if the creator has given you the power to do it then do it without any excuses, because excuses cause fruitless conclusions.

All that I'm trying to say is "Associate everything you love with love."

You guessed it. Love is always associated with peace, joy and abundant and fruitful life.

For love is Paradise.

When confidence is not enough, be Brave!

How to Make Your Travel Goals Happen

What about travel goals? What if your goal is to see the world? Again, we apply our steps which means we look at the kind of travel that we want to accomplish then work out a way to make it happen that is feasible considering our specific circumstances.

So we start again with visualization: picture the type of travelling you want to do, know what it is you want to get from your travelling and think about the different ways you can accomplish those broader goals.

Then look at your circumstances. What is holding you back? Budgetary constraints? Family responsibilities? Fear?

Then make your plan based on this information and break it down into small steps. Again, this might mean thinking outside the box and taking the 'non obvious' route to success. You don't necessarily have to take the obvious route by taking a gap year and travelling to various far flung reaches of the globe.

Alternative Travel Strategies

Perhaps you don't have the time or budget for that and would get just as much from travelling more locally? There are some incredible things to do and see in the South Africa also if you're in America, or if you're in Europe then you have the whole of the EU on your doorstep. This can present just as much adventure and variety and even if it's not exactly what you initially thought, it's still going to scratch that itch and that need for exploration and discovery.

Or how about just going for a shorter time? You can have a truly life-changing experience in just 3 or even 2 months. And you're much more likely to get a sabbatical lasting that long and be able to save the money. You can even change your strategy entirely and try taking lots of very small trips throughout the year. This might also be something that is easier to convince a partner of, versus going travelling for months at a time.

Money wise, you might be surprised at how little you need to travel if you go during non-peak seasons, if you stay on people's couches or if you use AirBnB. That means that you can earn a little money online to fund your travels.

Or how about asking your current job if you can be sent abroad? If the business has branches all around the world, this may very well be viable. Likewise, there might be a role that involves travel – or you could just apply for a job that involves travelling. That way, you travel while earning money and have a good explanation for your other half.

And there's no reason you can't take your partner with you either, of course.

*"FOCUS ON YOU UNTIL
THE FOCUS IS ON YOU."*

–

UNKNOWN.

CONCLUSION

It's time to make it happen no more excuses.

There are many more types of goals that you might choose to pursue and where you might choose to use this formula. For example, you might have goals that pertain to your finances alone, maybe to your property, maybe to your social life... perhaps your goal is purely to learn a particular hobby, or to improve the way you dress.

The whole point of this system is that it can be applied anywhere and when you do that, it will help you to really understand what it is you want and to make those aims concrete and tangible. This takes them from being dreams that you end up putting off forever and turns them into a series of steps you can use to make that happen. Sometimes this might mean reassessing your goals to make them that bit more achievable but if you're smart about this, they won't be any less rewarding. Maybe you can't be the next Brad Pitt or Angelina Jolie but there's no reason you can't start playing big parts in movies if you think about how to structure your life around auditions.

It's about knowing what you want and then assessing the quickest way to get as close to that ideal as possible. And as soon as you start trying, life becomes a whole lot more rewarding and amazing. It's time to stop dreaming and start doing...

It's time to make it happen!

"Blood, sweat and respect.

The first two you give, the last you earn."

—

DWAYNE JOHNSON

NOTES

<u>AUTOGRAPHS OF INSPIRING PEOPLE IN YOUR LIFE.</u>

www.ingramcontent.com/pod-product-compliance
Lightning Source LLC
Chambersburg PA
CBHW021222020426
42331CB00003B/430